Tigers
For Kid
Amazing Animal Books
for Young Readers

*By Kim Chase
and John Davidson*

All Rights Reserved.
No part of this publication may be reproduced in any form or by any means, including scanning, photocopying, or otherwise without prior written permission from JD-Biz Corp and
http://AmazingAnimalBooks.com. Copyright © 2015

All Images Licensed by Fotolia and 123RF

[Read More Amazing Animal Books](#)

Table of Contents

Introduction 4
About Tigers 6
Where Tigers Live 9
Tiger Features 11
How Tigers Hunt for Food 13
Predators For Tigers 15
How Tigers Communicate..17
The Social Life of a Tiger...19
The Evolution of the Tiger 21
South China Tiger..23
Bengal Tiger 25
Sumatran Tiger 27
Siberian Tiger 29
Indochinese Tiger 31
Malayan Tiger..33
Tiger Species That Are Now Extinct..........................35
Publisher 38

Introduction

Tigers have always been fascinating animals to watch. Perhaps it is the way that they quietly stalk their prey, as they gracefully move through the tall grass. Or maybe it is the long leaps they take when they pounce on their victim.

One of their most recognizable features is their bright orange colored fur and black stripes. But did you know that there is a reason for these black stripes? Do you know why the tigers have these black stripes?

You may know that the tiger is a descendant of the saber tooth tiger. But did you know that the tigers weren't always the size that you see today? Or do you know how many types of tigers exist today? Were you aware that a new species of tiger was identified and named as recently as 2004?

Are you aware that all of the tigers are on the endangered species list, and run a risk of becoming extinct? There are laws in place worldwide to save and protect these big cats. Some tigers live in very remote regions, and there is so much we still can learn about these amazing creatures.

Welcome to the world of tiger, as we explore the many regions they live in, and learn more about these powerful, skillful hunters.

About Tigers

The Siberian tiger is considered to be the biggest cat worldwide. By comparison, Sumatran tigers are among the world's smallest tigers. A tiger's size can depend on where they live, and the size of their food source that is available in their area. Tigers living to the North have been found to be larger than tigers that live in the South. Another interesting fact is that the northern tigers have coloring that is lighter than those tigers that live in the southern regions.

Tigers can be found in a variety of locations. For example, tigers living in the eastern Asia area experience climates that range from warm tropical swamps to cold temperatures. They can be seen in rocky locations, grasslands, forests and savannas.

Tigers are nocturnal (night) hunters. These large cats are meat eaters and can consume nearly 90 lbs. (40kg) in one meal! The tiger's stripes help to camouflage them in their habitat so that they can be kept hidden from their prey. Each tiger has their own unique striped pattern, with every tiger having a distinct set of stripes all of their own! These stripes are one way to identify the different tigers that may be seen.

Tigers are often found alone in the wild. Exceptions to this are when the female tigers are raising their young. It is rare to come across tigers assembled in a group. Should this odd event occur; then the group is referred to as a streak, ambush or a swift.

The meaning of the word tiger comes the word "tigris" which means arrow. "Tigris" is a Greek word. This Greek word can be traced further back to Persian origin, and a word meaning "arrow".

Six are the number of tiger subspecies that remain in the world today. All of these species are listed as endangered; with the Maltese Tiger considered to be the most threatened species of tiger. The Maltese tiger is also known as the Blue tiger because of their blue and black coloring.

The oldest remaining tiger fossils were discovered in different parts of China. These fossils are estimated to be approximately two million years old.

Some tigers have been known to kill humans. In fact, tigers kill more humans worldwide than any of the other cat species. One reason for this is that tigers are very territorial, and humans continue to enter into their areas of habitat.

Tigers are considered to be excellent swimmers. During the heat of the day, tigers have often been spotted cooling off and relaxing in the rivers, streams and ponds in their area.

Where Tigers Live

The area where tigers once roamed has been reduced drastically since the 1900's. Tigers can now be found in areas of Russia, China and Asia. With this reduction in space to live in, more tigers need to compete with what food is available.

Male tigers are very protective of the area that they claim to be theirs. To help them mark their territory, male tigers use their scent glands to spray the area that they are claiming. These glands send out a very strong scent, and act as a warning to other male tigers that they are in an area that does not belong to them. A male tiger can claim an area as large as 23 – 38 miles (60 – 100 km). A female tiger can claim an area as big as 7 miles (20 km).

A tiger has the ability to adapt to their environment. This is evident because of the many different habitats they can be found in. Their area to live in can range from open grasslands to the Siberian taiga to tropical climates and mangrove swamps. But in each very different region, the tiger is in need of three things if they are going to survive - water, cover and food. The tiger needs water to drink as well as give them a place to cool off during the hot temperatures of the day. They also need some type of cover so that their stripes can help them to blend into the environment, and give them a chance to stay hidden until they are ready to attack their prey. Tigers are also in need of food. They are skillful hunters, but need prey to feed upon.

Tiger Features

In general, a tiger's weight can reach nearly 670 lbs. (303 kg) and can measure almost 12 ft. (3.65 m) long. The tiger's claws can be almost 4" (10cm) long. The female tigers are smaller in size as compared to the male tigers. These cats are very fast as they hunt and stalk their prey. Because of the tiger's muscular build, it allows them to successfully hunt prey that is much larger than they are.

When you think of a tiger, one of the first features you may think of is their beautiful orange colored coat with black stripes. The black stripes are not only pretty, but they have an important job to do. These stripes are what allow the tiger to blend into the background of their surroundings. This is especially helpful when they are stalking their prey. Tigers need to stay hidden until they are ready to strike their prey. Every tiger's stripes are different. Because each tiger's stripes are unique just to them, it is one way to tell tigers apart.

A tiger has approximately 30 razor sharp teeth. Their claws have a protective sheath that shields them so they won't get worn down or exposed when the tiger isn't using them. The females' claws are smaller than those of the male tigers. Each foot has five claws, and tigers are often seen scratching their sharp claws into tree trunks. The width of these powerful claws allows the tigers to grasp and climb.

The tiger's back legs are longer than their front legs. This is the reason why they can leap nearly 33 ft. (10 m) forward at one time. Another feature that gives this hunter an advantage is their keen eyesight. During daylight hours, a tiger can see equally well as a human. However, at nightfall, the tiger's ability to see increases to six time greater than what a human eye can see. This gives the tiger a clear advantage over its prey. It is believed because the tiger has larger eye lenses and pupils, it enables them to see better at night.

How Tigers Hunt for Food

Tigers are meat-eating animals. As we have discussed, because of their large and powerful build, they can take on animals that are much larger than they are. But the tiger has to be smart about which animal to choose for its prey. For example, a tiger can bring down a bear or even a buffalo, but they will leave other animals alone. Tigers may search for weak or young animals, but will leave alone baby elephants because they know that they will be no match for the strength of an angry elephant parent.

Because tigers lack the stamina to travel for long distances for their food, they try instead to save up the needed energy for their hunt. First, they try to get really near their targeted prey before descending on it. With the help of their black strips to hide them in their surroundings, they quietly stalk their victim, and then pounce on them. It will take a tiger 20 tries before they are able to make 1 kill for their food.

Tigers usually search for their food at nighttime. Once they are successful in their hunt, they usually take their prey to a secluded place. Since tigers do not like to share their food, it is not uncommon for them to swim across water with their prey, or even take it up a tree. It is believed by some researchers that when a tiger has lost their ability to hunt in the wild, or no longer have the speed they need to catch their prey, this is when they may turn to area villages to do their hunting.

Predators For Tigers

Tigers are actually at the top of the food chain. Normally you would think that this should mean that they would have little to worry about in terms of predators. But the truth is that the very animals that they hunt can harm or even kill them. Although it is true that a tiger can take down a bear or buffalo or a younger rhino or elephant, these animals in turn could hurt the tiger so severely that the tiger will die.

All of these animals are very powerful. A bear has its powerful claws as its weapon of protection, and the strong buffalo can kick the tiger. If the tiger decides to take on a young animal such as the rhino, or the elephant, a tiger would not survive an attack from the parents of these animals.

Normally, the tiger would not even attempt to go after a young rhino or elephant, and would set their sights on a different prey. But when their habitat constantly grows smaller due to humans building or mining for minerals, they sometimes are forced to take risks in their search for food. The tiger's shrinking living area creates a problem for them. Now more tigers are after the same prey so there is less food to go around. Yet another situation that is very dangerous is a mother tiger trying to protect her young. She will fight animals that she would have otherwise avoided, risking her own life to save the life of her young ones.

How Tigers Communicate

Tigers can show many warning signs to tell other tigers to keep their distance and stay away. Some such signs could include arching their backs, and putting out their claws. A tiger is getting ready to pounce when you see that their ears are pinned back close to their head, there is a showing of their teeth, and their heads are held high.

If the big cats are just curious about something like other tigers or animals that may be nearby, then their ears would be up, and their tail high rather than in its usual low lying place. Body language such as this suggests that the tiger is feeling alert, but they are not feeling threatened.

One form of verbal communication used by tigers is roaring. Other tigers from as far away as two miles can hear the roaring of other tigers. These roars can act as a warning. Moaning is a second form of verbal communication used for gentle coaxing. Mothers may use moaning to let their young ones know to try something new, or to follow their directions.

The sound of snarling is used if the tigers feel like they may be in some type of danger. A mother tiger may snarl to keep male tigers or other animals away from her young. Hissing as well as snarling sounds can be heard if other tigers try to take food or share in the food of another tiger. Whereas the sound of purring could mean that the tiger is content. Since tigers live in remote regions, there is still much that can be learned as to exactly how tigers communicate with each other.

The Social Life of a Tiger

It is hard to fully understand how tigers all get along. Typically tigers live their life alone and do not like to share their food. However, there are times when male tigers will share their food with male tigers they are related to, or with female tigers that have cubs. Sometimes they will even share their food with other tigers when they recognize their scent. Those recognizable scents could from tigers that have been nearby. But this isn't always the case, and doesn't happen every time.

It is interesting to watch and see what happens when the male tiger decides that he will share his food. As is customary with other big cats, it is that the males that will eat first, and then share whatever is left over. When a male tiger has decided to share his food with female tigers and their cubs, they will let them either eat first, or allow them to eat at the same time that the male eats.

Much of the social activity happens between a mother tiger and her cubs. There could be anywhere from 1 – 6 cubs depending on the tiger species. It is not uncommon for there to be a dominant or leader among the cubs. It is this cub that will lead the way for sleeping and playing. Often times this lead role is a male tiger, but it can also be a female. As you can see, there are many things we can still learn about the tigers and how they live their lives, but the most important job to do first is to save and protect them.

The Evolution of the Tiger

When you stop and think about the tiger's early beginnings it is all quite fascinating. The earliest known tiger remains are estimated at being over two million years old and were found in China! These remains give us a bit of insight to the tiger and reveal some interesting facts such tigers were at some time a smaller sized variety than the tigers we see today. It is also believed that modern day tigers are related to a tiger that roamed the earth nearly 35 million years ago. This was the Saber Tooth tiger. Our current day tigers evolved into a subspecies that existed 25 million years ago. It is also thought that there were at one time many subspecies of tigers and that the South China Tiger is the one subspecies that tigers have evolved from. The day may still come when an important expedition can unearth fossils that can provide some additional information to researchers to give us all a better understanding of what types of tigers may have roamed the earth, and what they may have looked like.

The earth's surface was a very changing place 12 million years ago. Perhaps part of this surface change was the rising of the sea levels. Some of tigers became cut off from the other tigers. As a result, the Sumatran tiger's genetic species profile differs greatly when compared to the other tiger species. In order to survive, the tigers moved into different regions. It is estimated that it was nearly 12 million years ago when the Bengal Tigers entered India.

Today, there are six subspecies that exist. These big cats are the South China tiger, Bengal tiger, Sumatran tiger, Siberian Tiger, Indochinese tiger, and the Malayan tiger.

South China Tiger

The South China Tiger is considered to be the smallest of all the tigers worldwide. They are known for their strong orange color and beautiful black stripes. The stripes on this tiger are spaced further apart than on any other tiger species.

This is one example where the tiger's size is directly related to the size of its prey. In this case, a male tiger when it is full grown, can reach a size of nearly 8 ft (2.4 m) long, and weigh in at about 330 – 390 lbs. (149 – 176 kg). The females of this species are smaller than the males and weigh in at 250 lbs. (113 kg) and measure 7.5 ft (2.3 m) in length.

These tigers feed mainly on wild pigs and livestock. Feeding on livestock has caused a problem for both the tiger as well as for people. People have moved further and further into the areas where these tigers live and with bad results. People kill the tigers for eating their livestock, and the tigers have also been known to attack the people that live in these areas. Humans also hunted the South China Tiger for their pelts and bones. The tiger's bones are used in China to make medicine. In 1977, China banned hunting these tigers. It is a very rare to spot these tigers living in the wild. It is hoped that the South China Tiger has found a way to adapt and survive deeper in the forest region further away from humans.

Bengal Tiger

The Bengal Tiger is considered one of the largest of all tigers. They can be found living in India and Bangladesh. Their living environment can range from the heated desert areas to the cool and wet grasslands.

There may be many things that the Bengal and Siberian Tigers have in common. One possible reason for this is that DNA testing has revealed that 1% of the Bengal tigers are actually hybrids. This means that one of their parents was a Bengal Tiger, with the other parent was a Siberian Tiger.

Female Bengal Tigers are smaller in size than the males. The females can weigh about 310 lbs. (140 kg), while the males can weigh nearly 500 lbs. (226 kg). The heads on these tigers are larger than other tigers, and they also have tails that are very long.

The Bengal Tiger can eat approximately 60 lbs. (27 kg) at a single time. They feed on antelope, hogs, deer and buffalo. They have excellent hunting skills, and have been observed eating birds, monkeys, or other smaller prey when their usual food sources were scarce.

Sumatran Tiger

In the western part of Indonesia is an island known as Sumatra. This is where Sumatran Tigers come from. They are named after the place they live in. There are many facts that we can learn about these tigers. For example, the Sumatran Tigers have more hair around their neck, and on their faces than other tiger species. Also, their stripes are much closer together than stripes on other tigers. The reason for this is their habitat. The Sumatran Tigers live in an area where there is plenty of tall growing grass. Because of their stripes being closer together, it acts as an excellent camouflage for them, and they can blend easily into the background and surprise their prey.

Another interesting fact is the size of these tigers. They are considered to be smaller in size when compared to other tigers. Once again, it is believed that their smaller size is directly related to their environment. The area they live in, and their available prey are both smaller in size compared to other tigers. These tigers look very slender. The males can reach 300 lbs. (136kg) and measure 8 ft. (2.4m) in length.

The Sumatran Tiger is a fascinating hunter. One of the things they do when trying to catch their prey, is that they actually chase their intended victim into the water. This tiger is a very fast swimmer, and even has webbing in between their toes. Another ploy they use is to confuse their prey. On the backs of their ears, these tigers have "eye spots". These "eye spots" are actually white spots that look like eyes. These "eyes" are believed to keep the baby cubs safe from predators.

Siberian Tiger

As their name suggests, these tigers live in Siberia and are the largest of all the tiger species. These tigers can be found living far from humans in the higher mountainous regions, and feeding off of wild boars and deer that can be found in those thick regions of the forest.

Because these tigers live far from humans, there are very few reported cases of Siberian Tigers attacking humans. These tigers are very impressive in size, reaching 650 lbs. (294 kg), and measuring 10.5 feet (3.2 m) in length. These tigers are very fast as well as extremely powerful and strong.

Indochinese Tiger

What a mysterious tiger the Indochinese Tiger is! There is probably less known about this tiger than any other species! These tigers live in very remote mountainous regions far away from humans. They can be found in regions of China, Vietnam, Cambodia and Thailand. A full grown male can weigh between 330 – 430 lbs. (149 – 195kg), and measure anywhere between 8 – 10 ft. (2.4 – 3m) in length. The female Indochinese Tiger is smaller, and tends to weigh less than the males. The female tigers usually weigh about 290 lbs. (131 kg).

The Indochinese Tiger is often times mistaken for the Bengal Tiger. But here are some features to help you tell them apart. The

Indochinese Tiger has very narrow stripes, and a brilliant orange color.

One of the biggest threats facing the Indochinese Tigers is poaching. (Poaching means illegal hunting.) Although many countries around the world are trying to protect these tigers and many other species, poaching is still a very large problem. This is especially true for the Indochinese Tiger. One of the reasons for this is due to the fact that their bones and bodies have been used in China for centuries to make many different kinds of medicine. Their bones are made into powder that has been long believed to have special healing abilities. This need has created a huge demand for those tigers, and that is why poaching exists. It is also very difficult for the authorities to catch the poachers because the tigers live in such remote areas, and it is hard to catch them in the act.

Malayan Tiger

The Malayan Tiger is the newest recognized species of tiger to be named. It was in 2004, that this tiger became a recognized subspecies. This tiger is named after the place they inhabit, the Malayan Peninsula.

The Malayan Tiger is the smallest of all tigers, and because of its size and coloring, is often confused for the Sumatran Tiger. The diet of the Malayan Tiger consists mostly of deer and livestock. Because this tiger does feed on livestock, they are not welcome with humans. Once again, humans have invaded these tiger's natural living areas, and the result has been attacks on humans.

The people of Malaysia are very proud of this discovery of tiger species, and are working very hard to protect them. The name of this tiger has been the cause of great debate. Some people feel that rather than name the tiger after where it lives, it should instead be named after the person that brought this discovery about, and did the testing to prove the theory that there was another species of tiger.

Tiger Species That Are Now Extinct

AZERBAIJAN - CIRCA 1995 A stamp printed in Azerbaijan from the Flora and Fauna issue shows Caspian Tiger Panthera tigris virgata , circa 1995

It is important to know that conservation and protection efforts are being made to preserve tigers and their habitats. Tigers do face many problems in order to survive. In the wild, the prey they are stalking could fatally injure them. The places where they live are constantly shrinking due to mining, lumber projects, and people invading their living areas. The tiger's food source shrinks, and this causes the tigers to go hungry, or to take unnecessary risks in trying to find and get food. Hunting, poaching, and even poisoning the tigers all threaten their existence. There are efforts being made to try and preserve each species of tiger and save them from extinction.

Despite all the best efforts and conservation, there are some tigers that have recently become extinct. These tigers are the Balinese Tiger, The Caspian Tiger, and the Javan Tiger.

It was in 1937 that the Balinese species of tiger came to be considered extinct. Prior to that, this tiger roamed the Bali Island. These tigers were small in size. Their extinction was caused by a few reasons. First of all, there was no protection for these tigers in place. So hunting them whether it was for sport, for food, or to clear the area, was all considered acceptable. It is believed that none of these tigers were ever in captivity.

Extinction for the Caspian Tiger came during the 1970's. This tiger was thought to be a Siberian Tiger subspecies. For Asian people, the Caspian Tiger holds a special place in their culture. This tiger is displayed in their artwork, and written about in their literature. The Caspian Tiger has long stood as a symbol for strength, bravery, life and endurance.

During the mid 1970's, the Javan Tiger was sadly added to the list of extinct tiger species. This tiger lived on the Island of Java, and its extinction was brought about through hunting, and the destruction of their habitat. It has been reported that the last tiger sighting occurred in 1976, but there have been rumors and unconfirmed sightings of the Javan Tiger as recently as in the 1990s. Even with the reports of tiger sightings, it has never been confirmed just which tiger species may have been spotted.

Our books are available at
1. Amazon.com
2. Barnes and Noble
3. Itunes
4. Kobo
5. Smashwords
6. Google Play Books

Publisher

JD-Biz Corp

P O Box 374

Mendon, Utah 84325

http://www.jd-biz.com/

Tigers for Kids   Page 39

Tigers for Kids　　　　　　　　　　　　　　　　　　　　　　　　　　　　Page 40

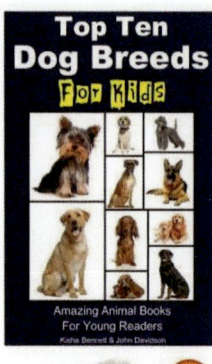

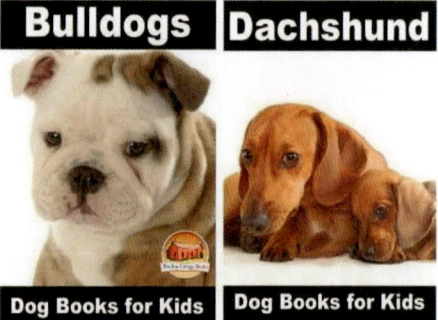

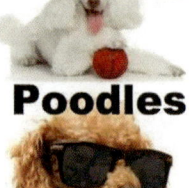

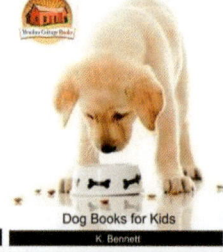

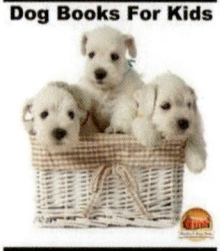

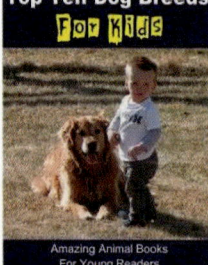

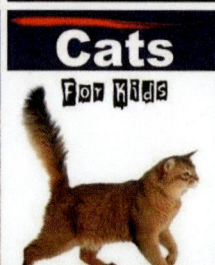

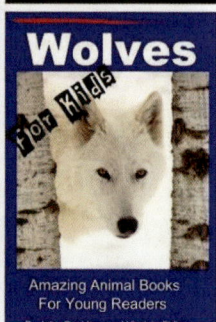

Tigers for Kids — Page 41

Tigers for Kids

Tigers for Kids — Page 43

Printed in Great Britain
by Amazon